Fleshed Out For All The Corners Of The Slip

Published 2021 by the87press

The 87 Press LTD

87 Stonecot Hill

Sutton

Surrey

SM3 9HJ

www.the87press.co.uk

ISBN: 978-1-8380698-9-6

Design: Stanislava Stoilova [www.sdesign.graphics]

You creatively reiterate declining fauna at the cusp of cosmic darkness. Water that blinds, shores that fail to elucidate their own boundaries. From these darkened articulations consciousness seems to rise of its own accord. Keep the language rising.
—Will Alexander

For the87press
Azad Ashim Sharma & Kashif Sharma-Patel

PROLOGUE TO THE IMMANENT VEX

impatient that we let the damned and wretched wave new circutry torn wasted driven on ends siding with the immanent vex in trabecular songs approximating stuttered oceanics/ unremitting wakes from fleshing the contact of sound unmade coming already met/ finally conscripting around its involution of new-new phase transitions when/ might just feel like finding other ways of lurks. shops opening shutters on to seasides we couldn't discern with our hands and a strip of air whips from essential to essential right down to this essence of evasion with the same interminable sky we love this something that we are at all/ strick in daylighting cycles and collexions. the night holds philharmonics we forget with the promise of a sea without terminus, far out from the familial subsmumations of an uncheckable key it surfaced until years later. farmyard overflows an expanse of planetary mains/ feels like coruscating an exsense we wear outside of ourselves for the life on track. listen instead for the elated skip, boldened, elastic. to seven blacks killed in a septet and more caught slipping in and out sing but here we're the ones that need help living how to see our emissions hum hell a lot colder and purely unrepeated. our residues brush animaterial, marauding a failed subjectivity lest the dead and dying smoke a personal orbit they pretend to dip/ outlast yr tug set/ overlay a more tabenacular beam but still give for u and yr friends iterant twilights/ yr the black night, doused levity, fish fish of an indigo rasa, staring blank aboriginal salt back, still clapping the same broad sways of high windrush outside our lanes and streets for one of the people's cracked anathemic songs saying true say we run upon how we sounded lyric for lyric like you think is that what you think? stepping yr way out of this poetry for what was left unsaid of yr sense of touch through feeling these sensations i can feel yr tares in our gilded fabric like granular scansion stress audible to remission, as lysed sentimental house and harbour for the immanent vex/ but must not/ nobody knows. crypt in resounding this echo of a black kid spitting an arial pleonasm/ makes in us an organising principle of our ruinous flooring teeth, skin, lip, nail, eyelid, breath and phosphorous/ more spit without making duppy and instead, when i don't know you but you must know who i am, sincapated plumes and shattered. in blockaids there's echo in compress. corners on corners lyric vex on long sequesters. black givenness taking us up in the clouds. liminal looks, ancestors enfleshed/ you can't see their 'flection's glare of sunlight rim they're too alloyed and all day artfully black boreal. blacklight visioning the same splitting of black action going to this place called nowhere fast and it's got to work. aeons and rhythms of work setting pace around the bits of anamorphological rhythms of work setting pace around the bits of grim shard ice. shadows barely viewed crossing blocked-off lays cresting a pure state lexis behind the curb. offshot and unprotected, still built to task /yet/ nobody made us. just roll back abiding, script a deadweight ride speaking an aporectic crowd in a burst out daydream on a rhododendron. can't then CCTV a slice of black worldsheet the way we lay of the land under streetlight /mystic/ arch

. . . the spirit whose letter we are . . .
—Nathaniel Mackey

. . . we breathe in that we rub . . .
—Fred Moten

Fleshed out for all the corners of the runaway moving across through

Drought with never having even thought of one of the suns

Or how things couldn't all be this resonating. Too bad for

Some or too well for giving back seen /what/ scathed and

Settled to when all ends were played for protection. Marooner then

Ark and flow into another key no later. Lower sequential E strumming a

Whole wall worth reticent about a corner, very clean choice into its meta on

Telephony, insofar as somebody has to stay and say what was

Thought of about how heavy the night long remonstrance was raining

Angelically amble when fissured. The unparalleled dead

Worrying each other's wrongs but was gonna be fine for the next one of us

Whoever standing in front and can't decide like once this

Other time, screw faced and increasing, inside tense where the other's

Lean in the residue of the aerated. Wading circumspectly for them to

Sleep in. From Hiroshima to Antigua and straight

Air by the throat. No resounding ether except with

Age as the concomitant, the beguiling fracture. Early sprigs of

Rain in the mezzanine. The current ineptitude of seasons rotating in part

Overstaying in the remaining threads of alchemy over this lightest ozonal

Zenith. Light light ecological split galvanic for the no later liminal like

Hands out more skits in more vanished and damaged. Thoughts of them and us

Mooring like sense us try and rot some sticks during night and dark. Where One

Can't challenge or war itself as self without their never been so much

Bad blood to bad it. With their being written or rid of it at points we

Assure it seeing it switch up the boat. Courtship thunder at the

Nose on boat. Sun quarter of the grain's scansion in the

Cornucopia. With the callous rigor of sunspots toiling the

Stratum of the black hand. The unlikelihood panoramic
voluptuously

Unfurling its vicinity of marshes. The unsounding viscous

Shorthand flowing from a nest of craters, not some

Serious cigarette smoke for a cool geological

Backdrop leaving us seriously eyeballing blushed nilon/ loosely

Clotted once again/ ran home.

Movements having moving moved a mysterium surfacing

Unmoving moved of impasse. Overturning to thoroughly

Unacquainted lunar freights. Outstaying the gone
euphonically depleted

Moors unimpressed with the turn surreptitiously longed for,
poorly

Anaesthetised on. Yielding remembers

Remaining. Bird seeds

Cuff no less

Quantifying in groves. Scumbled mirages of axle and codeine
slip

Capricious. Unfettered trills of wrecked lamentations
burnered and rumoured

Deeping again with an easier way out from home than
giving up on the

World in some verse to link us

Outside it. Who're you trying to understand when you

Listen to me. If you love me

Fuck with me and our deadness of night for things to (for)
get the

Words going

CAROUSEL (*redshift*)

'my ear against the ground, I heard Tomorrow
pass'

—Aime Cesaire, 'The Thouroughbreads',
Miraculous Weapons

'Aime
I surmise that the landscape was not a sum in itself
but the interactive plenum
between breathing'

—Will Alexander, 'On Higher Plugiston Current',
Spectral Hieroglyphics

look into redshift beaming us
walk rolling still stretched

out, still smoothing the
image of where we cut black

voicing, elliding all edging
out velvet reach and 'flecting redshift's

porous departures.
implacable fiburous rift, rioting

aurific scree without
when it sunsets. natural needing

natural/ say if
real recognise real. birdsong

the skyline, raised intonal and
alloyed freeing from the

straining steel yr closely
unheard jubilees, every cityscape

jump beat, yr
unrecursive collision again

eye enfolding cold aerations
witness of what we say of our

collapse and hiding in sync/ washed us
over. we could opal beam the end

of the night. loose the clamour our
friends generate. slip a lack of

passage together. this meeting of our
earliest moments singing

softly to me. nothing safer than these
moments drifting arial traces of

farmyard encased in windsweep.
cadences talking to you is talking

through you without
losing you feeling our

cold air distilling a
slow duppy's shroud in

neon highstreet octaves remaining
more caught in moonlight fray and

parting behind who we are that we
appear iridescent when we

look at the same clouds at night like
jet stream is how we

redshift at a distance like
large pearlescence

we had a foothold in this
touch of a sweet ethereal

essence at the same time earth no
longer splitting odourless

emission from given ex-
sensual after we spoke of us, yet

our shining crests the blackest
runaways screaming warped more and

more how i want to feel already
alive with the clasp of the slip of

some of yr other long connected ruin, still
retaliating kicked across maximum

barring, everywhere redshift bleeding
hints, curved and curving the

timeline, carouselling where we
mist above seeing us down resounding some

mucky phono-optic blue murder/ we could
go on into old night. back and you back

before none of us still could step to the pier's
edge preing what looks lovely but it's our

futurition here ruggish blank believing, tenouring
our absence of truly unaccustomed

redshifting under dark deck of dubplate. sliced
ice up a nerve ensipirts the wrist because

inexpressibly full with what words can do to
time/ hearing the immaculate weave from

redshift nothing like redshift beaming us,
spinning us black, circumgathering a mantra/ high

rings clearing indirect tense across chordless.
shades of its glean late on a schooner replete

on the verge hiding a bleached negative back
ahead to pure words you come down on/ no

names to show us hearing
decantations pouring airs lapping

tinctures. we look out from small
shrills i imagine us laughing all our

angles turning over the midnight
size. break maroon flesh like

air yr profile locked ruseing
real together cold palms that

can't grip/ clasps clean and
air tight, glossed lowly, evincing

nothing coming over us. wind blown
dying starlight heights down to the

gleanest block tip edged to
crack the ways our staring

leisons black bodys like slapped
hardened but dull integuments. ancestral

smoke-filled room climbing blunt park
rigs grades dark as any day we walked

home passing as a mystic
forest's stowed away and legged

out heartache for makeshift studio shorns/

faux ice to set the bits of
redshift pressing down on us in a real

run in plain dark sight/ black lit
scrolling/ risen like piecing

together unreal mind ret/ pulse but its
concrete, noxious, preeming. 'frain

for the dead out friends back to the
gleenest carousel/ high floor

raids on our lysed
hems in duffle form. cold

gold metallic night to touch from
when we used to prang a

sixteen (bar) in the red when it was heard black
surf speaking a warm compress in

threes and twos with no insides, not anymore
looking at anything we leave behind but

ever prevading parallax/ oceanic inner
sounding like ocean prays itself/ leave for

jungle reema lording eski looking for
crisp, searing tet thru the coldest airs we

speak between recollections only to come
back to yr breeze past me. trance resonant

stare on speaker phone back back along
sheafs that plane laid cast mystic

wisp inside us on friendly street for
9 hr long whereabouts unknown left

alluvial, scattershot, like sea
bream glaring unseeable waves of

garms that we redshift under our
breath at the doors of the dance ret

minded, lacey, suffering terra
earth sagaciously being

purely obsidian trace, inseparable teeth
chain and ring/ lyrically shots our

change, money, exchange, money/ parse
storming, gloss tet caught in the throat/ wet

release and charge of tone light. a small
copse on the fly conjectures wild

flays of missed elegiac or soft inocous
tug on coptic nerve. birch trees

shining a forest staccato fading above
songbirds, daylighting, fleshed out, no

ancestral pauses/ if you think im real i
take my timing to yr big dead, echoesless

even zeel/ you, we, shadowing
secret police moving seeing us

dying taken for dissipated rich
gestation of stomas, spinning us

black, angulating out-from small
roes the edges showing nothing

restored. set back or
dematerialisation. coptic sense of

air enfleshed. ghostly crowned
apogees. mystic heart

break. redshift
repetition the distance

sweapt and flipped what we
didn't tell

still dark wash gushed us,
spinning us black

ethereal
dreaming that we

crossed short-
circuiting all

cadences of the
heart beat no

change to the word's
untimely

bussing that we hear
us from all ends of

the visceral clamour
in single myriads un-

seen from when we made
realness forever return burst

baseness of verse to
link us outside without

running on a
pull up in the

darkness leading
deep enough to

get us lost in
remaining in whole arrays

of sun, carrying inside us
each celestial

movement without
change making us

see change all along
remembering our

share of coalescence.
what are we to

look at, and how
saying it won't

figure a line of
flight, jade of

fluidity pon
air we dress in glints

of sunset. eye's touch water's
humming mid-

drift out of
focus, rotates its

pulsations, so much
history just

settled there as an ark
leveling suite of denuded

sea greens into
fuscia pink f

majors breaking
live notes and

looks away like
surf. evidence of

things not seen as
black blue

vermillion/ deck of
flesh over

dusk in its already
dawning, dust

kicked up dawning
with only tertiary

gleans to signal
dying seen woven into

the impossible seen
stirring our

siphonophores/ diasporic
at the same time

seeing us in our lofty
auriginary leave, roving

where we are all the
way to this thing

dispersed. round here
we got our

place in the
sun saying

even then
what happens to

our straining
to feel. leaning

seeing wind inbetween
the oppressed/ times gone

spurious around
sameness of exhaustion/ conjectures

of detritus that we
breathe from their

dry phores an
ashen finesse. we

hosts of their memory's
high water, mineral echoes

of grief, can't
help but

fall in and
out the

dark
wash together

held up
jettison away

from self
snaring, couldn't

get away whispering
ultramarine knowing

full
capture in

escape. no more
sacred in the

small outside that
no one else

heard the system
in the stoma. none

listened in
for love but for

apotheosis/ rewrote the
blank, indeterminate

main. fleet of
foot through

stone yr
marsh   meadow wood   unlike

daystar   ritual ritual still
life the

fuck the police   a black
body is sacred

everywhere leaving no
clues   unlike

daystar   ritual ritual
still life the

fuck the police   a dead black
body is sacred

everywhere leaving
no clues   raised

interlacing sheets of
sleet ice in the

iris under a
deep rift

Notes on Aural and Aura

'Poetics: flight across precipitous intransigence.'
—Will Alexander, *Across the Vapour Gulf*

'Black experimental *writing* begins at the point where (white) notions of the avant garde become impossible, or at least irrelevant. Against the defining opposition between meaning and form in European aesthetics— where the former is always on the side of conservation, reaction, tradition, etc.—let us begin by saying that *Black experimental* writing refers to a body of texts where this opposition is at once superseded and rejected.'

—David Marriott, 'Introduction: Black Experimental Poetics', The Black Scholar, 47:1, 1-2.

'We are now arriving in the crackling fields of metaphor.'
—Aime Cesaire, *Lyric and Dramatic Poetry, 1946-82*

ˈ

Aural (adj); 1844 'pertaining to the ear,' from Latin *auris* 'the ear as the organ of hearing'; meaning 'received or perceived by ear' is attested by 1860

Aura (n); from Latin *aura* 'breeze, wind, the upper air [ether],' from Greek *aura* 'breath, cool breeze, air in motion,' from PIE *aur* from root *wer* 'to raise, lift, hold suspended.'

1

Aural and aura here are conceptualised as metaphors of and for non-relationality in black experimental poetics. This is to initially suggest that what they image does not reflect back to us the subject-object relations that galvanise black experimental poetry's predisposition to forms of institutional life, given in literary critical, literary aesthetic discourse; neither, here, do they constitute the re/production of the relation between content (contained within the text) and form (present to the subject's conscious faculties), which are conventionally necessary for the structural interpretation and comprehension of black experimental poetry, presupposing its consignation to the objectivity of the reader's subjective experience.

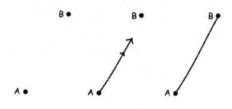

Such 'recourse to metaphor'[2], following Nathaniel Mackey, given in aural and aura, 'betrays an estrangement, a distance, that the metaphor—the word is derived from a verb meaning "to carry over"—seeks to overcome.'[3] The black poet's estrangement conditions its estranged connection to what is 'indescribable and indeterminable.'[4] And so I want to conjecture that aural in aura, in their mixed metathetic metaphoricity, are non-relational. They do not relate to each other as separate images or nominalised modalities for representing existents, but are animated, enlivened and enfleshed by each other without mediation (in space), and neither as events (in linear time). They neither assert, ascend, nor affirm the point at which black experimental poetics comes to be definitively understood as a form which

---

[1] This is a basic representation of relation in Euclid's *Elements*. A and B are two distinct points separated by the space between and around them. They are not related except by way of the straight line which could represent linear time, historical progress (etc.). My thinking is that A and B are kept separate(d) and different(iated) (which could also be to say mediated) by the line (relation): relation=difference+separation; relation differentiates and separates things by way of space and time.

[2] Nathaniel Mackey, *Discrepant Engagement: Dissonance, Cross-Culturality and Experimental Writing* (New York: Cambridge University Press, 2009), p. 176.

[3] Nathaniel Mackey, *Discrepant Engagement: Dissonance, Cross-Culturality and Experimental Writing*, p. 176.

[4] Nathaniel Mackey, *Discrepant Engagement: Dissonance, Cross-Culturality and Experimental Writing*, p. 176.

itself, subsequently, precludes in reading, invoking Aime Cesaire, black experimental poetry's poetic music; precludes in the sense of black experimental poetry's de-, and the same time re-composition (or the double-decompositionality) of its externally and internally imposed forms of musicalisation in to sound and air.

Such mixed-metathetic-metaphoricity instantiates the disclosure, given in the movement of a lytic breakdown of its external poetic structures, of a musicality in black experimental poetics. Its outcome is of an inexplicable but constant, repetitious proliferation of a moment—both actively futuritive and inventive—that is 'from a greater distance than sound'[5] in which, invoking Fred Moten's, would be of a musicality in poetry, or a black poetic experimentality.

The black experimental poet is configured as the twofold, dialectical-phenomenological object of contemporary poetics. Their configuration in discourse produces, in the transcendental subject, a problematic encounter that troubles the stable, intuitive invocation of the work's context. I want to conjecture that what Moten might call the black 'social life of [experimental] poetry'[6] uphends itself, in experimental practise, from the spatiotemporal contours of the transcendental subjectivity, thereby complicating literary criticism's hermeneutic suspension and nominalised suspicion of the black poem (presupposed to be without life), forcing

<hr>

[5] Aime Cesaire, *Lyric and Dramatic Poetry, 1946-82*, trans. by Clayton Eshleman & Annette Smith (Charlottsville: University of Virginia Press, 1990), I v i.

[6] Fred Moten, *Stolen Life: consent not to be a signle being* (North Carolina: Duke University Press, 2018), p. 168.

their forms of critical (and aesthetic) engagement up against the aporetic horizons and experiential limits of the blackness of the black poet at the level of an individualising, individuated reading.

The black social life in poetry corresponds to the acute dissolution of the subject's spatiotemporal sense of embodily coordination with the external world of physical phenomena. Which is to say that the relation between subject and object, through which the transcendental subject's prepossession of ideal objective forms, coercively prefigures its hold, by way of perception and intuition, on black life as an existence predisposed to the rational, conscious faculties of the individual subject.

That relationality undergirding how subjects and their objects are represented as experiential and embodied structures a critical impetus in poetics that overdetermines the communication of a discursive language that precludes, and so keeps separate, emanations of black poetry's animaterial, enfleshed decomposure in its recombination of a musicality's 'phonic substance'[7] of the poem that is without and actively resists form, that is prior to the appearance, for the subject, of the black poetic text as a corpuscular, isolated phenomenon.

What can be gleaned from black experimental poetry's consubstantiation with the black poet's experimental

---

[7] Fred Moten, *In The Break: The Aesthetics of the Black Radical Tradition* (Minneapolis: University of Minnesota Press, 2003), p. 35.

modalities of expression from the position of being an impossible subject is the interexchange of elemental, non-physical air and breath at the level of the very black sociality of its recitations, speech acts, and utterances. As in/corporeal, black experimentality *in* poetics galvanises the effusion and emission of the black body. As fleshed out, that body is unmade, no longer a bodily reference to an individual subject's presence; not obliterated but made into an element, air or breath, as black poetry's condition of im/ possibility for, and refusal of subjecthood.

Poetic music is *of* the black sociality (rather than relationality) of the poem, but is not imaged corresponding to the strictures of a discursive language on poetics. Being *of* is not only before, in being infront of us, but being *as* that aural (sound) and aura's (breath) condition of emanation and content of black poetic life. Neither object or phenomena, its proliferation of sonic animateriality, black poetry's anafoundational aura(lity), the music that sounds/ fleshes out the totality (rather than the universality) of black social life in poetry, has affectability as its porous modality of enfleshment. This is (the) sound of flesh, invoking Mikel Dufrenne, as black experimental poetry's 'affective *a priori*.'[8]

The fleshing and sounding out of unmade breath becomes a medium for, and the content of feeling, which itself corresponds to the condition of

---

[8] Mikel Dufrenne, *The Phenomenology of Aesthetic Experience*, trans. by Edward C. Casey (Illinois: Northwestern University Press, 1973), p. 441.

animation, the state of being animated regardless of distance or location without submitting the black poet to the nominal position of a progenitor of the felt dimensions of black experimental praxis in the domain of subjectivity. The felt presence of animate content in black poetry, of an animaterial element (sound, breath) actively disimbricating the relation between content and form, subject and object, text and reader from these categorical nexes of contemporary critical poetics, does not gesture to the profusion of a specific black experimental poetic material that, as such, would be predisposed to subject's capacity to transcend black poetry's earthly iterations of life in its experimental modes of emanation and animation.

Aural and aura's social immediation of and through feeling entails the fleshing, sounding out of a corpus, giving and being given by new expression(s) to what we, as critically and aesthetically engaged subjects undergo in being given over to the double-decomposition of poetic form's signifying orders of meaning, representation, and value. The critical substance and scope of these *Notes* runs concomitant against (and over) institutionally paradigmatic forms of poetic discourse on black experimental poetic life given as a sociohistorical category of literary thought and production whose practical aims intend to relate the text's lines of interpretation and comprehension that can be applied, in order to continually refine what Moten might call 'arbitrarily virtualised'[9] forms of reading.

---

[9] Fred Moten, 'Music Against the Law of Reading the Future and "Rodney King"', *The Journal of the Midwest Modern Language Association*, Vol. 27, No. 1, 1994, p. 57.

2

What Fred Moten calls *The Music*[10] informs aurality's (the voice's) 'generative-organisational structure, a paradoxically anarchic principle of totality'[11] that black experimental poetic thinking underscores, in its relation to literary discourse, in its refusal of a 'reduction [...] to individual voice.'[12] *The Music* might be commensurate with the music of poetry which Cesaire tells us 'cannot be external or formal'[13] insofar as what animates black poetry, gives it life (which, in this usage, is also to presuppose its decay), 'is transferable but not interpretable from either inside or outside'[14] the text (as object) or

---

[10] 'This term is most immediately an echo of the title of a recent book of Amiri and Amina Baraka's *The Music* (New York: William Morrow Co., 1987). Their title refers specifically to that music which is overwhelmingly the creation of African-Americans, though the complex indeterminations to which the racialization of music is subject (despite the quite determined racial conditions in which the music is formed), renders "The Music" an inoperative synonym for "Black Music." There are at least a couple of reasons why "The Music" is a proper noun too complex and general for its own good: the term immediately exceeds itself since it gives itself over to the action, the making of the music, which is at its heart and it refers to the organizing principle which enacts, finally, a very precise deconstruction of its own internal structure—the dialectic of noun and verb, effect and action, music and its making—which seems to operate as a kind of unity-in-duplication. But it is the fact of the term's irreducibility- its refusal to be contained by any of the possible definitions which, in fact, it contains that makes me want to retain it.'

[11] Fred Moten, 'Music Against the Law of Reading the Future and "Rodney King"', p. 53.

[12] Fred Moten, 'Music Against the Law of Reading the Future and "Rodney King"', p. 53.

[13] Aime Cesaire, *Lyric and Dramatic Poetry, 1946-82*, I v i.

[14] Fred Moten, *In The Break: The Aesthetics of The Black Radical Tradition*, p. 179.

reader (as transcendental subject); incomprehensible but responsible for infusing and transforming[15] black social life from and as an ostensible corpus, cut off from any vital impetus, into and with what Cesaire might call 'the flesh of the world's flesh'[16], into and with the felt, affectable sense (*empfindung*) of the *givenness* that is black experimental poetry's mode and content of impossibility of being an object for a subject. What is given is fleshed out over and against what Moten calls the law of reading. He writes that the

> 'law of reading is not the activation of an interplay reading itself and the interpretive system it constitutes and by which it is constituted. It is, rather, manifest in a certain doubleness outside of this deconstructive process: a process in which the intermittent oscillation between deconstruction and the complex of its others fosters an artificial interarticulation of methods, styles, idioms, within which not only the text of literature but the idea of totality are disappeared.'[17]

The law of reading adduces an alignment with its attendant law of transcendence that not only

---

[15] Fred Moten, *In The Break: The Aesthetics of The Black Radical* Tradition, p. 179.

[16] Aime Cesaire, 'Notebook of a Return to My Native Land' from *Aime Cesaire: The Collected Poetry*, trans. by Clayton Eshleman & Annette Smith (Berkeley and Los Angeles: University of California Press, 1983), p. 69.

[17] Fred Moten, 'Music Against the Law of Reading the Future and "Rodney King"', pp. 51-52.

presupposes a subject which thinks its text into existence, but also one that garners the individual right and capacity to conserve its subjectivity by way of a certain de(con)struktion, which is to say a calcification or nominalisation, not only of the text's lifeworld (*lebenswelt*) but its composite, animaterial existence which permits of no strictly ontological or epistemological account of itself as the self-evident, self-referential means for the subject's apprehension of the de-, re-compositional work of the black poetic text.

The disappearance of black poetry is not paramount to the disappearance of poetic music, or *The Music*. Disappearance is not only fugitive, maroon flight from the hegemony of future readings, but is also disappearance into the black social life of poetry hiding in plain sight in that we can hear and speak (of) its disappearance as giving off, emanating or out-flowing (the) textual ecology of sonic elements—pushing back in its dissipation into air against black experimental poetry's subsumation under, and calibration with such a transcendental category as a *form* of discursive life that disaffects its modes of living in relation to the institutions of literary criticism and literary aesthetics.

Aural and aura—more than articulating points of traversal in black experimental poetics of the duality between inside and outside that bear no structural necessity to the relation between the subject and their object—spreads out away from the possibility of ideal experiences that would culminate in the self-discovery of an interior basis for self-expression represented by, and representable to a principle of poetic form as the sociocultural construction of (its) practical applications.

They (aural and aura) galvanise without demarcating the critical and aesthetic aporias or limits of an intuitive perception of black experimentality in poetics which precludes, in thought and experience along discursive interpretations, sense impressions of its potentiated feelings or latent animations of the text as a manifold thing among other ramified things— an object in 'all its mobalised richness'[18] invoking Cesaire, wherein its cultural-historical moment, at the level of its constitution of an identifiable subject formed and produced within a historical form of life (contemporary poetics), induces at or on its limit, invoking David Marriott, a 'moment of *inventiveness* whose introduction necessarily never arrives and does not stop arriving, and whose destination cannot be foreseen, or anticipated, but only repeatedly traveled, and, therefore, not future at all'[19], an arrivance without arrival, a condition inhering in black experimental poetics of remaining in a state of only ever being about to exist.

---

[18] Aime Cesaire, *Lyric and Dramatic Poetry, 1946-82*, I v.

[19] David Marriott, 'Inventions of Existence: Sylvia Wynter, Frantz Fanon, Sociogeny, and "the Damned"', *CR: The New Centennial Review*, Vol. 11, No. 3, 2011, pp. 53-54, my emphasis.

3

'We speak of our corrupt institutions so that
they can be reformed. To speak of our corrupt
institutions is, in fact, to reform them.'
—Stefano Harney, Fred Moten, Denise
Ferreira da Silva,
All Incomplete

I'm interested in conjecturing the animaterial
substance of/that is black experimental poetics's
'formal incompletion'[20], its interstitial emanations of
things and their actions out from within the infinite but
bounded space of the voice initially, here, understood,
invoking Moten, as 'flesh's aeration, its more or less
than circular breathing [...] in its differentiation,
exposure, flight and flay.'[21] The voice casts the flesh of
the body (which is the corporeal world of the individual
subject) off into (the) irretrievable air, the black
ether that J. Kameron Carter and Sara J. Cervenak
theorise as 'unfettered ur-matter, unthinkable
exorbitance, and deregulated transubstantiation'[22]
or, as I'm inhering, the black social life of poetry's
irreducible, imperceptible affections of and from
improvisation (of aurality, flesh sounded out, flesh
the animateriality of sound) and invention (of black

---

[20] David Marriott, 'Inventions of Existence: Sylvia Wynter, Frantz Fanon, Sociogeny, and "the Damned"', p. 73.

[21] Fred Moten, 'Black Topological Existence' in Arthur Jafa's *A Series of Utterly Improbable, Yet Extraordinary Renditions* (London: Serpentine Galleries & Koenig Books, 2018), p. 17.

[22] J. Kameron Carter & Sarah Jane Cervenak, 'Black Ether', *CR: The New Centennial Review*, Vol. 16, No. 2, 2016, p. 204.

aurifice, the galvanisation of the black life of poetry without form or external presence) upon which the black life of poetry moves as the emanation of poetic music/*The Music*, not as the transcendence of lived experience, and beyond either the communication and/or immanence of its own sociality. 'What is at stake when black flesh fugitively undulates into and as ether and in so doing, un/makes the world itself?'[23] J. Kameron Carter & Sarah Jane Cervenak ask: 'What might it mean to think about blackness as enacting an un/making, as enacting amid regimes of settlement an unsettling that is also an un/holding, a release of self from its entrapment within property into an alternate intimacy?'[24]

Within what Moten calls the law of reading, black experimental poetry is often read as an extension of a communicable, intersubjective entity that garners the capacity and sovereign right to pass and form a consensus on, and discursive insight into the textual ecology of black poetic content and forms of experimental practise. The animate liveliness of black poetic experimentation—which is neither the constituent or product but emanant outcome of the experimental practice of black sociopoetic life that is, to the transcendental subject, without critical or aesthetic boundaries and limits *before* (infront, in the presence of) [the law of] reading—unfounds (1) the underlying objectivity that establishes the poem's intelligibility as a textual manifestation of the subject's social and historical becoming, as well as (2) the

---

[23] J. Kameron Carter & Sarah Jane Cervenak, 'Black Ether', p. 204.
[24] J. Kameron Carter & Sarah Jane Cervenak, 'Black Ether', p. 204.

context of its relation to the institution's subsequent overdetermination of the telos of past and future emergences of critical, aesthetic readings of a black poetic text's significance to the cultural-historical phenomenon of contemporary literary discourses on poetry—readings concealing and enacting its de(con)structive interplay of phonic substance, that will have already (but not always) precluded black experimental poetry's transgression of the literary discursive modalities of, and protocols for reading.

Trangession is understood, here, as lytic (disintegrative and abating) and decreative. Following from Simone Weil's definition of decreation as 'making something created pass into the uncreated'[25], lysis and decreation are the experimental affects of black aura(lity), the poetic condition of black poetry's givenness, its immediation of content and/*as* modes of living that are inexplicable to the transcendental subject morphic desire to form and produce its world from raw, unformed material sense data.

Speaking of a black experimental poet, a figure predisposed to the relationality founding discursive communicabilityandthereproductionofinstitutionality in communities of knowing, recognisable, sovereign subjects as, invoking Edouard Glissant, the 'nonbeing of Relation'[26], as relation's 'impossible completion'[27], is not so much to suggest its absence from literary

---

25 Simone Weil, *Gravity and Grace*, trans. by Emma Crawford & Mario von der Ruhr (London: Routledge Classics, 2002), p. 32.

26 Edouard Glissant, *Poetics of Relation*, trans. by Betsy Wing (Ann Arbor: University of Michigan Press, 1997), p. 187.

27 Edouard Glissant, *Poetics of Relation*, p. 187.

critical, aesthetic forms of representation, but to the obscure/d life of the black experimental poem that surrounds the textual ecology of poetic discourse as the simultaneously overlooked and extractive field of forms of institutional life, insubstantially evidenced by its sonic/enfleshed permeation out from within the spatiotemporal coordination of subjects in relation to their objects in the encounter with the text's figuration of the black poet as a thing without reference to its existence.

Relation reinstantiates space and time as a priori fundaments for the transcendental subject's mastery over their lyric intentions. When dialectically-phenomenologically confronted with the phantasmatic figuration of a black subject as *its* nonbeing, this is undone from 'outside of relation.'[28] Non-being is what I am conjecturing to be what Moten calls the impossible subject, predisposed to poetics as the creative principle of form and of lyric subjectivity but, again, without itself achieving the status of formal objectivity, with no discenrable limits at the level of the subject's literary imagination. Without limits, they are NO-BODIES (incapable of communicating a stable, subjective coroporeality), following Denise Ferreira da Silva by way of Moten, 'whose existence spreads beyond the juridical borders of any given state and the ethical borders of every nation'[29], and whose subsequent disclosure

[28] Edouard Glissant, *Poetics of Relation*, p. 187.

[29] Fred Moten 'History Does Not Repeat Itself, but It Does Rhyme', in *After Year Zero: Geographies of Collaboration* ed. by Annett Busch and Anselm Franke (Warsaw: Museum of Modern Art in Warsaw, Haus der Kulturen der Welt and Authors, 2015), p. 201.

reveals the constructed phantasm of an autonomous black poet, functioning as a transcendental category of and for thought, given *in already being given over* to expressions of lyric subjectivity as a creative, embodied act of sovereign individuality, moves 'by way of its [the lyric subject's] own degradation, is enthralled by its own irreducible vulnerability, incompleteness, decay, which it enacts at the intersection of expansion and expression, the constant violation of its own integrity, on impulse.'

Lyric subjectivity becomes instrumental for the self-preservation of ethical life within the state that NO-BODIES problematise and threaten, put into question. The conservation of the proprietary existence of an individual life, by way of the lyric subject's passing through, receiving and disseminating earthly, diagregated iterations of subjugated life and living, autoimmune by its ideological perceptions and sovereign fantasies from the state's coordinated destitution of black people(s), is what NO-BODIES give conceptual challenge to against their 'externally imposed determination [as non-self-determining], as there for and under the dominion of a masterful subject whose capacity for reason and reflection allows him not only to suppress or subordinate his own impulses and appetites but also obligates him to control those who are supposed to have no such capacity.'[30] Moten continues:

> 'The masterful subject is privileged and obligated to control all that shows up for

---

[30]Fred Moten 'History Does Not Repeat Itself, but It Does Rhyme', p. 201.

him in the world of things. On the other hand, things are without impetus and have no internal volition. They are affectable. The paradox is that the affectable ones must immediately be considered dangerous in their supposed lack of armeture precisely because the condition of affectability is contagious given the irreducible desirability of affectbility's indecsreet non-being. This is to say that affectability, which is the essence of social life, is the condition of possibility of desire, as such. What can be more terrible than bearing the projection of affectability as the primary object of the impossible subject's desire and fundamental instrument of the impossible subject's disavowal of desire? What could be more dangerous than the constant enactment of the subject's impossibility. What could be more beautiful than this insistent indiscretion given in and as the fleshing out of this general and generative affectability.'[31]

Affectivity as essence, in the sense of *empfindung* in that NO-BODIES in their nonbeing feel, touch, and are animated through sensation, profligate moments of immediacy admitting no prior relationality (that differentiates and separates), is how givenness, the mode and content of impossible subjectivity,

---

[31] Fred Moten 'History Does Not Repeat Itself, but It Does Rhyme', p. 201, my emphasis.

becomes 'more + less than the construction of sovereign power.'[32] The intentionality of the lyric subject transubstantiates the animaterial [breath, flesh] of the black social life of poetry from a nexical, nonsentient corpus into jouissance. There is no exchange, invoking Roland Barthes, of the *grain*, conceived as an element not solely contingent upon the law of reading's de(con)strutive interplay between meaning and signification, that Barthes tells us 'is the body *in* the voice'.[33]

The grain of the voice makes no immediate or neccesary deference to the subject who speaks or listens (to other subjects embedded in, or reading out a text). What is adumbrated in black experimental poetry publically performed or privately recited, is the grain's future imperfection, invoking Marriott, the indeterminate crystallisation of aura(lity)'s phasic composure and recomposure and decomposure, without ever eliding, of [the elemental grain of] black poetry's 'inaudibly specific difference'[34] on the one hand, and on the other hand, following Will Alexander, its 'resonant aural poetic.'[35]

---

[32] Fred Moten 'History Does Not Repeat Itself, but It Does Rhyme', p. 202.

[33] Roland Barthes, *Image, Music, Text*, trans. by Stephen Heath (London: Fontana Press, 1977), p. 188.

[34] Fred Moten, 'Music Against the Law of Reading the Future and "Rodney King"', p. 53.

[35] Will Alexander, *Towards The Primeval Lightning Field* (New York: Litmus Press, 2014), p. 63.

4

'There is an imaginary in music'[36] Barthes writes, 'whose function is to reassure the subject hearing it [...] and this imaginary immediately comes to languages via the adjective.'[37] The law of reading ensures the adjective's 'economic function'[38] as a descriptive and prescriptive predicate or structural rejoinder, that it remains the 'bulwark with which the subject's imaginary protects itself from the loss which threatens it. The man who provides himself or is provided with an adjective is now hurt, now pleased, but always *constituted*.'[39]

Being constituted by language means to emerge as the product of a particular sociohistorical form of life. The literary subject constitutes their being constituted according to a relationally linear, teleological, wholly monodimensional and monodirectional (or intentional) reading along the linguistic structures and ontoepistemological paradigms (for being present at their own knowing and being) of *their individual subjective experience* of black experimental poetry when read, listened, spoken, or performitavely demonstrated. But that poetry's experimentality, at the level of its phonic substance, its sonic emanation, does not emerge, is not presenced, in the known future as that which

---

[36] Roland Barthes, *Image, Music, Text*, p. 179.

[37] Roland Barthes, *Image, Music, Text*, pp. 179-180.

[38] Roland Barthes, *Image, Music, Text*, p. 179.

[39] Roland Barthes, *Image, Music, Text*, p. 179.

comes before that which can be foretold, which is also to say foreclosed in being foreheld, in and by reading, but *lingers* out-*from*-within the moment or event, conjured by reading, of its own sociohistorical phenomenon.

The Music here is formative neither of the imaginary of a transcendental subject, nor an impossible subject imagined as its future anterior, or its felt, experiential fact without evidence. It (*The Music*) itself resounds in poetry how its social life, or perhaps more precisely its social(ly) aurific breath, is fleshed out in giving over and being given over to the real impossible enactment of sovereign, transcendent, lyric subjectivity in black poetic experimentality's 'improvisation of the gap/chiasmus/caesura/cut'[40] that traverses, the 'oppositional ways in which we encounter the world, namely, prescriptively and descriptively'[41], normatively and nominally, as the law of reading's overdetermination of black experimental poetry and the musicality of its poetics as what Edmund Husserl might call the spiritual product of transcendental(ly) intersubjective relations grounded in and by the pre-objectivity of language. What is at stake, then, is the permeability of black experimental poetic life that exists neither as relational, nor communal, that is, in the absence and/or excess of mediation, but as movement without change, which is to say without violence in literary discourse language's (pre-)objectification of [forms of] life

---

[40] Fred Moten, 'Music Against the Law of Reading the Future and "Rodney King"', p. 60.

[41] Fred Moten, 'Music Against the Law of Reading the Future and "Rodney King"', p. 57.

Weil writes that we 'participate in the creation of the world by decreating ourselves.'[42] The creation of the world without an act or acts of will, as a possibility to enact an 'earthly, subjectless'[43] existence galvanises, without introducing to the world of the self, 'modes of unknowable enfleshment and unseizable life'[44]: fleshed out unmade sound, gone to the flesh of the earth in the black poet's 'radical refusal of a point of view in favor of a general inhabitation and enactment of a view from nowhere.'[45] Like Weil says: 'We must be rooted'[46], not as beings but as existent things, 'in the absence of a place.'[47]

---

[42] Simone Weil, *Gravity and Grace*, p. 33.

[43] Fred Moten, 'Black Topological Existence', p. 15.

[44] J. Kameron Carter & Sarah Jane Cervenak, 'Black Ether', p. 205.

[45] Fred Moten, 'Black Topological Existence', p. 15.

[46] Simone Weil, *Gravity and Grace*, p. 39.

[47] Simone Weil, *Gravity and Grace*, p. 39.

5

To speak of the image, or metaphor of *The Music*, here, is to be comported not so much to being embedded in forms of life but, again, to linger, by way of and through the *labour*[48], or in the immersion of black aura(lity)'s sonorous, aurific emanation and fleshly in/corporeal animation of black poetic experimentality. If *The Music* can be conjectured for a moment as the active context (and so not itself a context) of that experimentality, it is

---

[48]Labouring and/as lingering, conjectured from Karl Marx's notion of living labour, discussed in his *Grundrisse: Foundations for a Critique of Political Economy*, attempts to gain insight into the relational dynamic black experimental poetry is fused to the generality and generativity of 'subjective wealth'. which doesn't infer individual persons defined in relation to what they produce but to the circumsrcibed forms(and relations) of withholding, here, black poetic content (flesh, sound, breath) that is structurally precluded from achieving the status of subjective expression, interred by an objectivity in and as its separation, 'as the law of [...] exchange between capital and labour', to 'general wealth' . . . Living labour exists as both raw material, or what Marx calls 'absolute poverty: poverty not as shortage, but as the total exclusion of objective wealth', and at the same time as the active impetus of and for 'general wealth (in contrast to capital in which it exists objectively, as reality) as the *general possibility* of [wealth], which proves itself as such in action': 'it is not at all contradictory', Marx writes, 'that labour is *absolute poverty as object*, on the one side, and is, on the other side, the *general possibility of wealth* as subject and as activity'. It is a real contradiction given in the separation, the division, of labour from itself in and as the production of objective value into capital and wage labour as a function of social and cultural modes of production. Objective forms of capital realises the individualisation of commodities in which general wealth 'may be tangibly brought into the possession of a particular individual' that can be commodified for a particular use.The contradiction glimpses the real expressed interanimation of the separation between the living, 'not-objectified' (i.e., *actually existing material* of) labour and the dead labour of capital, reduced in and to the notion of poetics (as in poiesis) as the creative principle underlying its servile predisposition to the generativity of forms of relation (which is to say difference(s) and/as separate(d)) that the law of exchange, given a second time in the law of reading, galvanises between poverty (as objective) and wealth (as subjective).

the im/palpable placelessness that its sound galvanises and enfleshes, carries over (indicating a traversal, an emanate out-flowing) in blackness's dissolution, following da Silva, of 'the whole signifying order that sustains value'[49], which she describes in its twin modes as the effect and the equivalent of both 'determinacy'[50], consolidating value in its '*determinate*'[51] relations and forms (capital, discourse, categories) 'marked by effectivity (efficient causation), that is, relations marked by power differences insofar as one element effectively acts upon another'[52]; as well as its '*determinant*'[53] capacity or tendency to be [that] 'form which is applied to matter'.[54]

That 'crime against poetic music'[55], Cesaire tells us, in which its musicalisation refigures dialectics and transcendence as both the distantiation of poetic music from the positive, or objective structures of life (conceived as containing innate value), and its redeployment into the machinations of, say,

---

[49] Denise Ferreira da Silva, '1 (life) ÷ 0 (blackness) = ∞ – ∞ or ∞ / ∞: On Matter Beyond the Equation of Value', *e-flux journal*, No. 79, 2017, p. 9.

[50] Denise Ferreira da Silva, '1 (life) ÷ 0 (blackness) = ∞ – ∞ or ∞ / ∞: On Matter Beyond the Equation of Value', p. 9.

[51] Denise Ferreira da Silva, '1 (life) ÷ 0 (blackness) = ∞ – ∞ or ∞ / ∞: On Matter Beyond the Equation of Value', p. 9.

[52] Denise Ferreira da Silva, '1 (life) ÷ 0 (blackness) = ∞ – ∞ or ∞ / ∞: On Matter Beyond the Equation of Value', p. 9.

[53] Denise Ferreira da Silva, '1 (life) ÷ 0 (blackness) = ∞ – ∞ or ∞ / ∞: On Matter Beyond the Equation of Value', p. 9.

[543] Denise Ferreira da Silva, '1 (life) ÷ 0 (blackness) = ∞ – ∞ or ∞ / ∞: On Matter Beyond the Equation of Value', p. 9.

[55] Aime Cesaire, *Lyric and Dramatic Poetry, 1946-82*, I v i.

capitalist forms of relation that represent black musicality in black experimental poetic life, in its non-objectivity, as being the absolute poverty of (as and in) subjective wealth, as that which has no innate value but is predisposed to external forms and modes of value creation, which characterises the law of reading's 'manifest[ation] in the commodification and fetishisation of illusory finished products [...] which are, in the end, easily identifiable effects of intellectual labour in the capitalist order'.[56] Moten continues:

> 'The conditions of that labour inevitably result in readings suspended between homogeneity and heterogeneity, succession and continuity, event and context, and mirror, quite unsurprisingly, the global, multinational capitalist system from whence they come. Our work must diagnose and avoid the spirit of (that) system and we must, I think, be attuned to the fact that such a task has everything to do with how you sound.'[57]

---

[56] Fred Moten, 'Music Against the Law of Reading the Future and "Rodney King"', p. 61.
[57] Fred Moten, 'Music Against the Law of Reading the Future and "Rodney King"', p. 61.

6

Poetic music's 'aural inscription(s)'[58] moving decreatively, which is say lytically, in nonabidance with the sign's psychic morphology—corresponding to the subject's intentional formation of meaning in the world from discrete, privatised objects appearing to and represented by way of consciousness—tenders the [condition of] impossibility of judgement and intentionality to reduce (in form) content to its mode of appearance (whose *appearing that also appears, its givenness,* it cannot inter) within the transcendental subject's construction of life in ethical, valuable terms that is already contingent on the metaphysics of its own emergent causation.

The image of *The Music*'s poetic music is the image of the black poet not as a self-individuating, corpuscular, embodied subject but porously unbeholden to (but not unburdened by) the morphic representations and internal formations of external appearances, as poietic making. A nonbeing outside of space and time not as *a priori* fundaments for any subjective experience but as an image without content, an X that, against a certain Kantian notion of judgement as both the transcendence and/that reveals the limit of the world, representation as both illumination (of knowledge) and erasure (of its material conditions), 'overthrows all the laws of thought.'[59] Judgment is consrained, here, by the law

---

[58] Fred Moten, 'Music Against the Law of Reading the Future and "Rodney King"', p. 62.

[59] Aime Cesaire, *Lyric and Dramatic Poetry*, I i.

of reading's attendant laws of the 'law of identity, the law of non-contradiction, the logical principle of the excluded middle'[60], being coterminous with the prescription and descriptions of the black social life of poetry in terms of its debasement from literary discourse, and receding, crossing, suspending, rejecting [the law of reading's] forms of judgment.

The image spoken of does not formally represent black poetry's musicality in literary [critical, aesthetic] discourse (and the intersubjective communities they produce); nor does it function as the privileged idiom yoking black experimentality and social poetics to what the subject can communicate, transcend, and identify through their experiences of the text as the generation and re-presentation of their sociocultural conditons in relation to forms of capitalist, institutional production; it [the revolutionary, distant image] endures through a movement—at once lytic and decreative, profligate and unfounded—that is articulated (rather than communicated) in black experimental poetic's distantiation from, which is also to say its poetic musical refusal of, literary discourse's nominalised (historical) and contextualised (social) logics of exclusion that veils (through the category of contemporary poetry) the animate, emanate, fleshly, animaterial sociality of black experimental poetics, the black life as a practise of impossible subjectivity, precipitating neither as historical (dialectical) or revelatory (phenomenal).

---

[60] Aime Cesaire, *Lyric and Dramatic Poetry, 1946-82*, I i.

7

Contemporary poetry's veil(ing) of *black* poetic sociality 'reproduces the effect of power [...] [rendering] racial emancipation contingent on the obliteration of racial difference'.[61] Nathanial Mackey writes that the 'very effort to talk down [racial] difference [...] underscores the tenacity of [...] racial polarisation'[62]: Racial difference configures the black poetic subject as being indubitably present to the very mediated literary imagination (conjured in experience as being without mediation), and remains thus, the ontoepistemological constituent for the transcendental subject's critical and aesthetic construction of thought as *its* product of the sociocultural matrix of productivity that it, in turn, has formed in intersubjective communion.

When Cesaire writes that 'Poetic knowledge is characterised by humankind splattering the object in all its mobilised richness'[63], the difference that is the object of (dialectical-phenomenological) protocols for investigating what appears in conscious experiences by way of the senses, i.e., thoughts, is ramified, which is also to say deferrential to the law of reading's object—the future—and aim—cultural differentiation which, invoking da Silva, 'rests on the

---

[61] Denise Ferreira da Silva, *Toward a Global Idea of Race*, (Minneapolis: University of Minnesota Press, 2007), p. 8.

[62] Nathaniel Mackey, *Discrepant Engagement. Dissonance, Cross-Culturality and Experimental Writing*, p. 253.

[63] Aime Cesaire, *Lyric and Dramatic Poetry, 1946-82*, I i.

principle of *separability*[64] that 'considers the social as a whole constituted of formally separate parts. Each of these parts constitutes a social form [of discursive life], as well as geographically-historically separate units, and, as such, stands differentially before the ethical notion of humanity, which is identified with the particularities of white European collectives.'[65]

It is not only, or not so much, that the object of reading, along the discursive trajectory of contemporary poetry and poetics, *is* racial difference; it is that difference *as* an object of *its* separation of [blackness as] race from discursive forms of life (literary criticism) stands in for what is read and written as a form of life's overdetermination of blackness's predisposition to lyric subjectivity, as the black poet's a priori modality of unifying, which is say universalising, that obscures the very 'resonances and agitations at work in the text' producing a black experimental poetic text's '*animated incompleteness* whose components tend toward as well as recede from one another, support as well as destabilise each other'.[66]

'The music itself breaks […] But the music also mends itself'.[67] This animated incompleteness names aurality's improvisational and inventive, lytic and decreative interstical breaking and mending in and of *The Music*

---

[64] Denise Ferreira da Silva, 'On Difference Without Separability', ed. by Jochen Volz & Júlia Rebouças for the 32nd Bienal de São Paulo - Incerteza Viva (Live Uncertainty) (São Paulo: Fundação Bienal de São Paulo, 2016), p. 63.

[65] Denise Ferreira da Silva, 'On Difference Without Separability', p. 63.

[66] Nathaniel Mackey, *Discrepant Engagement: Dissonance, Cross-Culturality and Experimental Writing*, p. 258.

[67] Nathaniel Mackey, *Discrepant Engagement: Dissonance, Cross-Culturality and Experimental Writing*, p. 176.

given in the *givenness* of poetic music. The 'life-giving'[68] and 'life-ending'[69] aura (breath) of the black social life of poetry, which expresses poetic music's disagriation of blackness from its racialised compartmentalisation in lyric subjectivity, the lyric subject's mastery over its relation to the world and its sovereign right to grasp it through individual expression. But aural and aura, poetry's auratic, aurific flight and dispersal from an external and formal superimposition of raciality, clad to, and encoded in the law of reading and its discursive forms (criticism, aesthetics) of institutional life that produce literary categories and the subjects to elucidate them, goes out, over, the sociohistorical phenomenon of difference *as* separation (as relational) that structures raciality as the abstraction of blackness that galvanises the lyric subject's transcendence towards universal expressivity and, instead, attends to

> 'a poetry that would mark and question the idiomatic difference that is the space-time of performance, ritual, and event; a poetry, finally, that becomes music in that it iconically presents those organisational principles that are the essence of music. The thing is, these principles break down; their break down disallows reading, improvises idiom(atic difference) and gestures toward an anarchic and generative meditation on phrasing that occurs in what has become, for reading, the occluded of language: sound.'[70]

---

[68] J. Kameron Carter & Sarah J. Cervenak, 'Black Ether', p. 205.

[69] J. Kameron Carter & Sarah J. Cervenak, 'Black Ether', p. 204.

[70] Fred Moten, *In The Break: The Aesthetics of The Black Radical Tradition*, p. 44.

ACKNOWLEGMENTS

A draft version of 'Prologue to the Immanent Vex' first appeared in the87press's digital poetics series on their online open-access platform *theHythe*, run by the Director of the87press, Azad Ashim Sharma and Head Editor, Kashif Sharma-Patel (15.10.2020); a draft version of 'CAROUSEL (*redshift*)' was included in *There are New Suns / Bruised Blossoms*, a publication edited by Andrea Maria Popelka and Kunstraum Niederoesterreich that accompanied the exhibition *Life constantly escapes* (26.02—03.04.2021) curated by Andrea Maria Popelka, as an extension of their series *L/XVE*, at Kunstraum Neideroesterreich, Vienna, Austria; sections of 'CAROUSEL (*redshift*)' were drafted from a creative-critical poetry and poetics workshop entitled *On Lysis* that I lead with the Nottingham Contemporary for their poetry series, *Five Bodies*, curated by Sofia Lemos alongside Dr Sarah Jackson, Dr Linda Kemp and Dr Jack Thacker, and fasciliated in collabortion with Nottingham Trent University and the University of Nottingham (09.12.2020); *Notes on Aural and Aura* was initially a paper I gave at the School of Advanced Study, University of London (under a different title), for the Contemporary Innovative Poetry Research Seminar series organised and run by Dr Amy Evans Bauer (University of Kent) and Professor Robert Hampson (Royal Holloway, University of London) (30.09.2018); the title poem 'Fleshed Out For All The Corners Of The Slip' was read as part of *Break Into The Forbidden*, a poetry reading fundraiser organised and hosted by Sarah Shin, editor of Ignota Press that was raising money for black liberation organisations and bail funds in the support and service of justice and resistance movements in the US in the wake of the murder of George Floyd (05.06.2020).

'CAROUSEL' - Travis Scott

'The Projects Pt. 2' - Prem

'Raid' - Prem

'Bruiser' - Babyfather

'Hmm' - Loraine James

'Cut 'Em Off' - Dizzee Rascal

'Wisdom Eye' - Alice Coltrane

'A Love Supreme, Pt. IV - Psalm' - John Coltrane

'GOD' - Kendrick Lamar

'Radhe-Shyam' - Alice Coltrane

'Moon Rays' - Pharaoh Sanders

'Watrfall' - IAMDDB

'Moonlight' - IAMDDB

''Roll With Us' - Doja Cat

'Why' - Mary Lou Williams

'Sweet Earth Flying - Pt. 5' - Marion Brown

'Newham Trio' - Footsie

'Dust' - Duval Timothy

'Shell of Light' - Burial

'God Hour' - Babyfather

'Collect' - Klein, Diamond Stingily

'Say So' - King Tubby, Augustus Pablo

'Sweeter Than A Savage' - BbyMutha, Mohammed El-Kurd

'Misty' - Dorothy Ashby

'Wild Is The Wind - Live at Town Hall; 2004 Remaster' - Nina Simone

'Strange Fruit' - Nina Simone

'Running' IAMDDB

'Passages' - rRoxymore

'Still' - Skepta

'The Realness' - Babyfather

'Set It Off' - Reeko Squeeze, Carns Hill

'Aquafina' - Bali Baby

'Roses' - BbyMutha

'Bialero' - Sonny Sharrock

'Prema - Live' - Alice Coltrane

'Inclined' - Eartheater

'Peripheral' - Eartheater

'Passage' - Vijay Iler, Wadada Leo Smith

'as long as ropes unravel fake rolex will travel' - Dean Blunt

'Clocking the game (Enter a new atmosphere)' - Novelist

'When There Is No Sun' - Sun Ra

'Chetu' - Bengt Berger, Don Cherry

'The Music Is A Sound Image' - Sun Ra & his Arkestra

'Robyn' - cktrl

'As Far As The Eye Can See' - Matana Roberts

'So Long' - SusTrapperazzi

'Divine Love' - Wadada Leo Smith

'Weds in Cali' - Novelist, SusTrapperazzi

'Misty Cold' - Ruff Sqwad

'With That (feat. Duke)' - Young Thug, Duke

'Deh Deh' - Unknown T

'Nappytex' - Blue Iverson

'Po' Boy' - Bukka White

'Hell Hound On My Trail' - Robert Johnson

'Hand Drops' - Loraine James

'Saw It Coming' - Wiley

'Ave verum corpus' - William Byrd, Ora Singers

'Aisha' - John Coltrane

'Black Ting' - Loraine James, Le3 bLACK

'My Future' - Loraine James, Le3 bLACK

'Whatsapp' - Duval Timothy

'Hope Dealers' - Klein

'MUGU' - Dean Blunt